colorcats

colorcats

By Margaret Gates Root

Book One

ʌʌ M ʌʌ

Clowder Books

ISBN 978-0-9968995-0-5

Printed in the United States of America

colorcats.org

This book is dedicated to the best cat ever . . .
yours.

*The drawings in this book are presented in
landscape style, with the binding at the top of the images,
so they're friendly for left or right-handed colorists.*

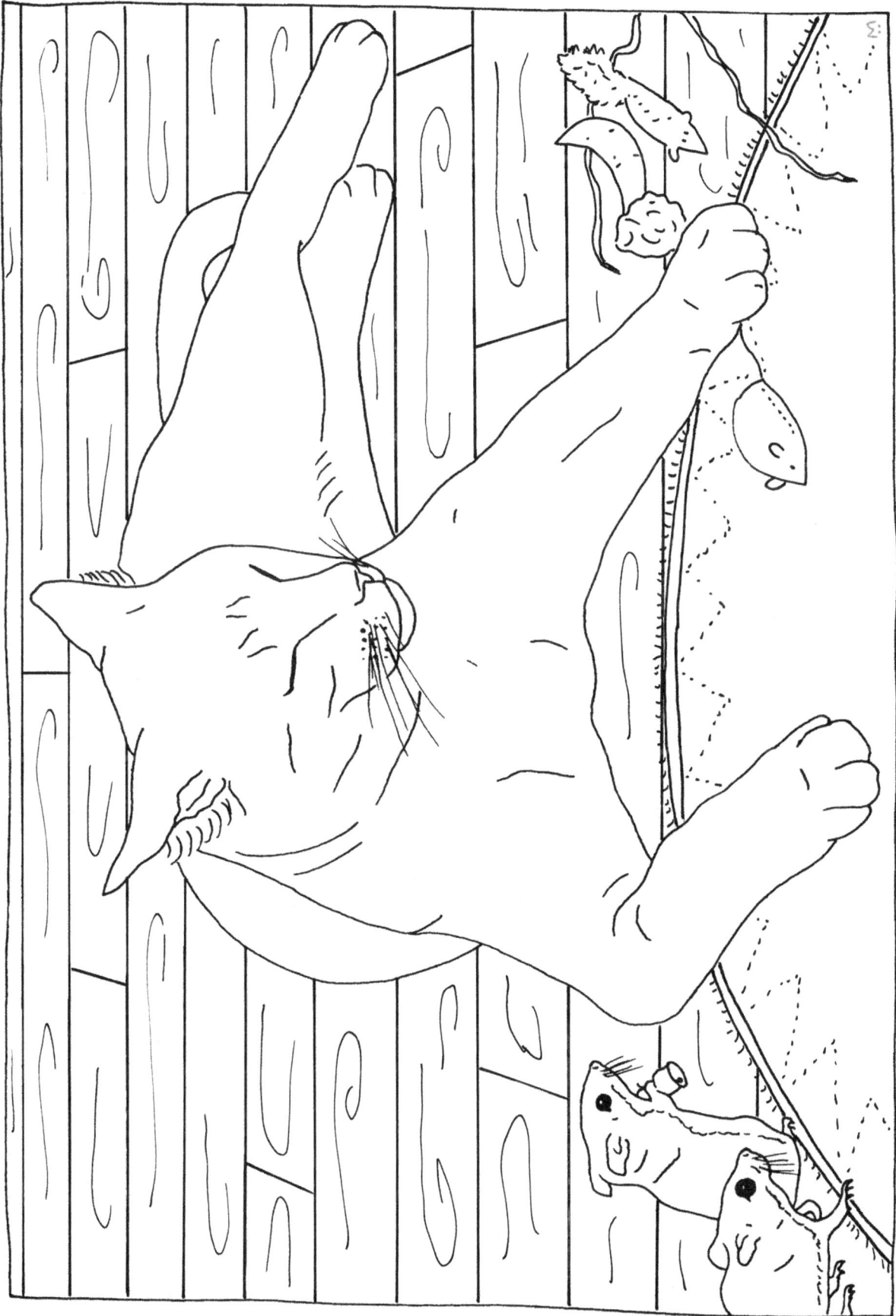

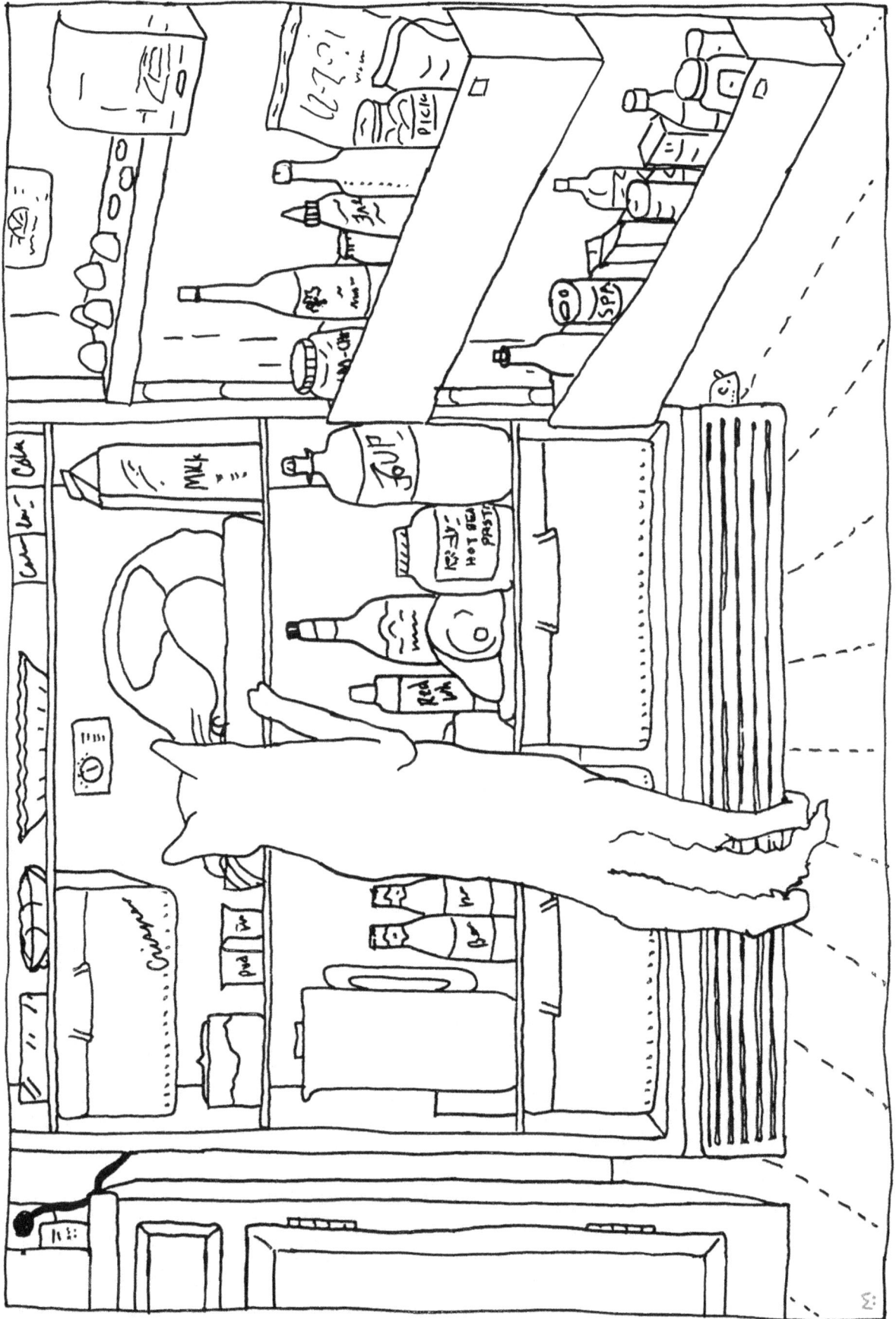

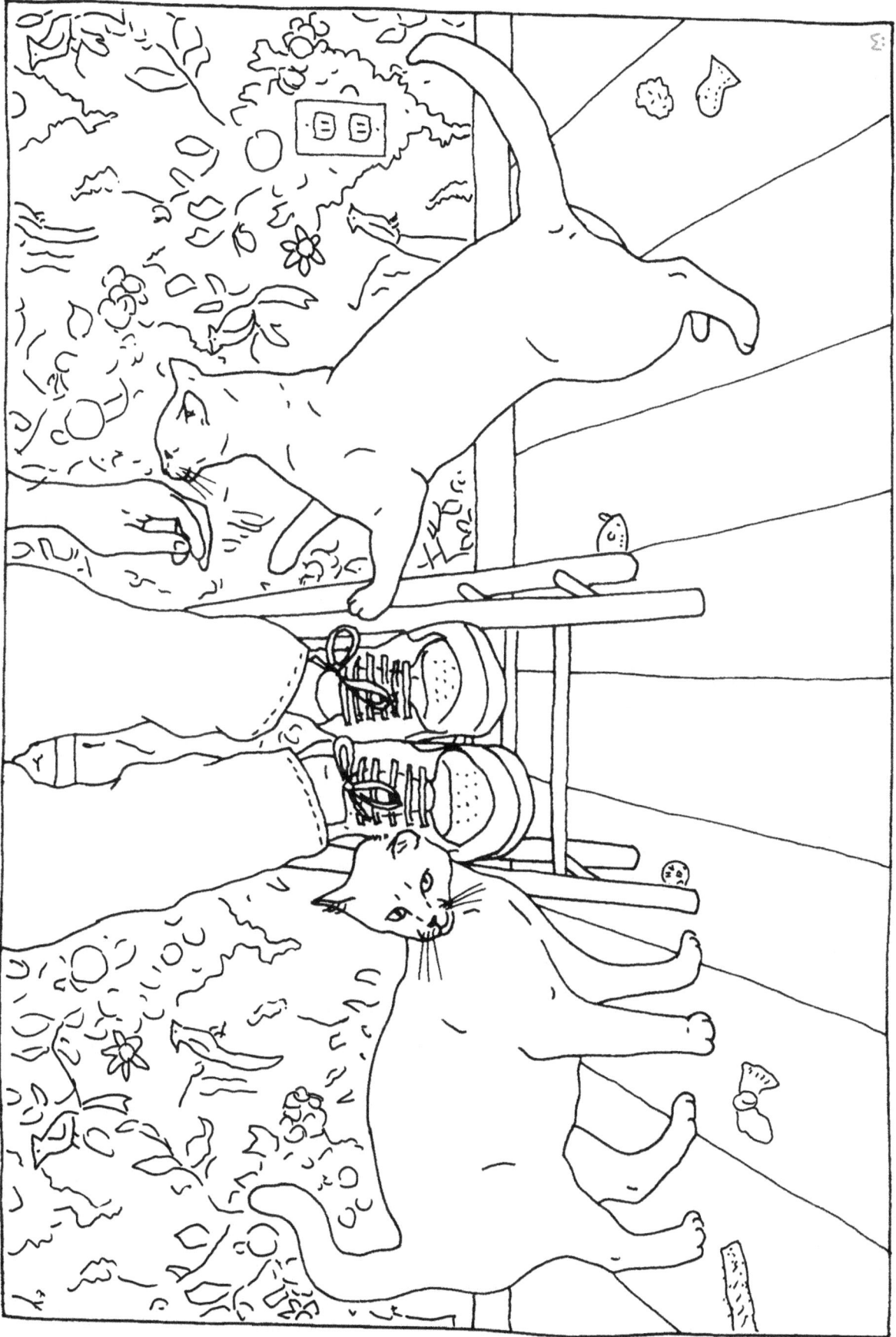

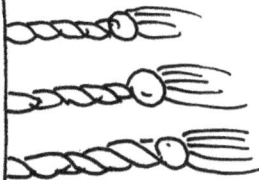

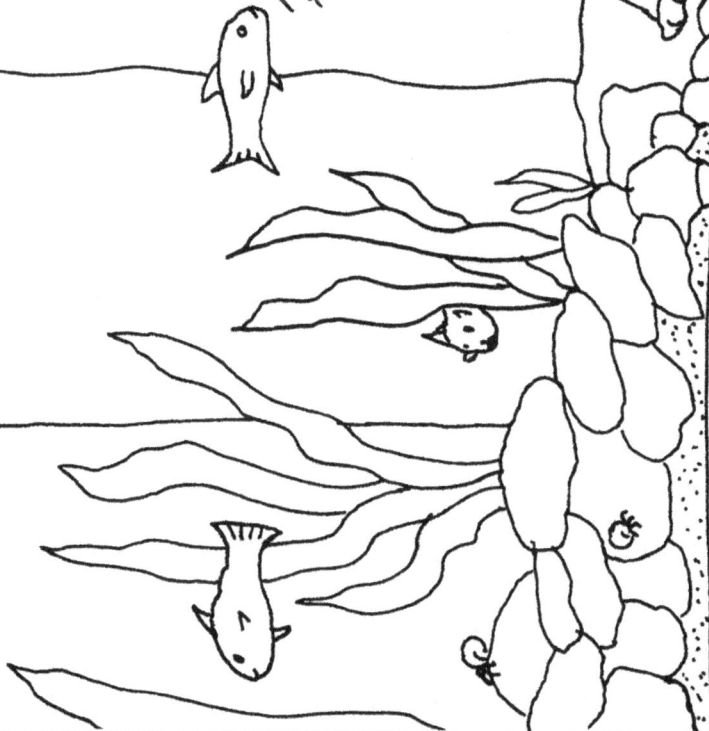

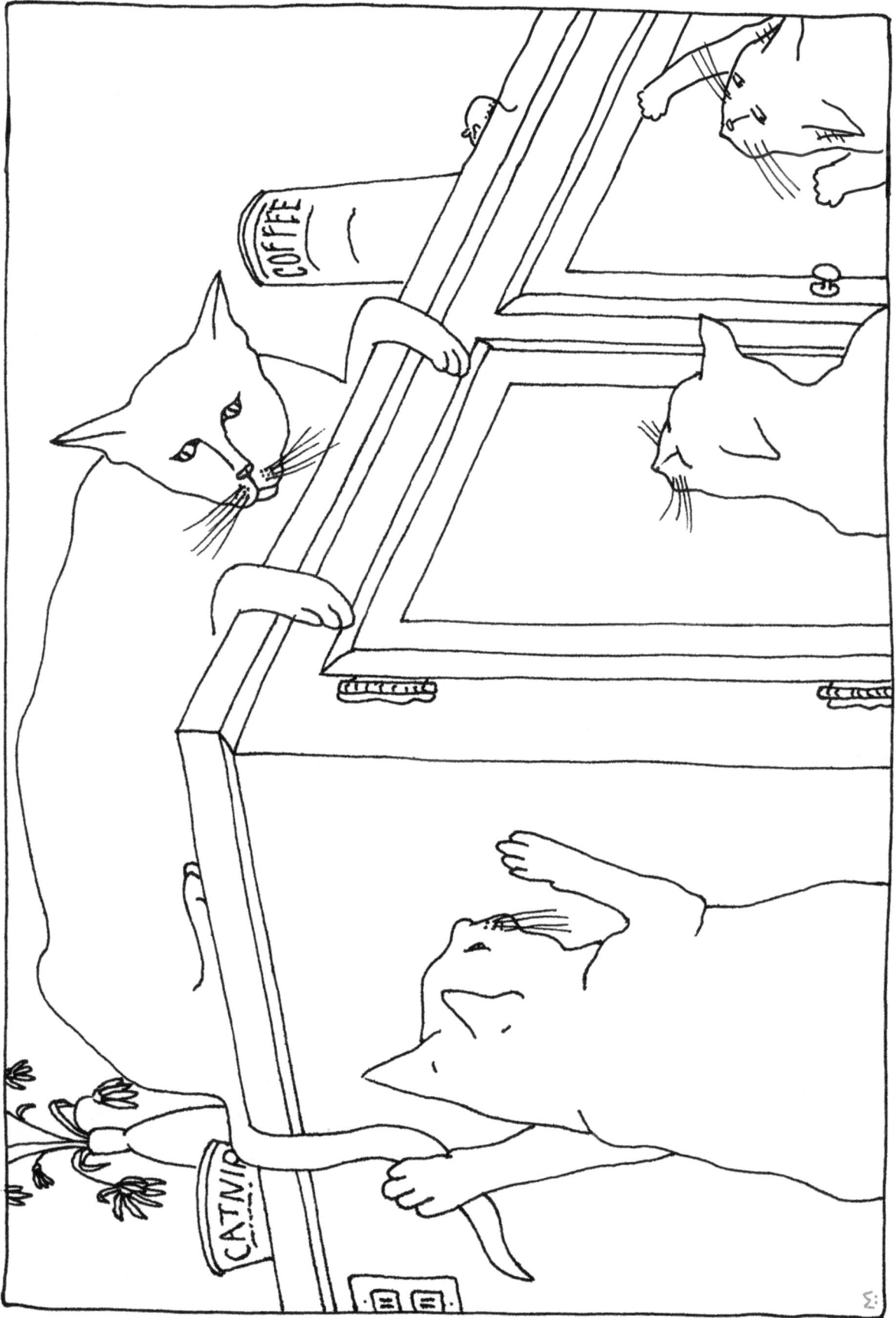

SALTED BLACK BEANS
wesson
Soy
Sesa oil
Chili
Bambo
TOFU
Chili peppers
RICE

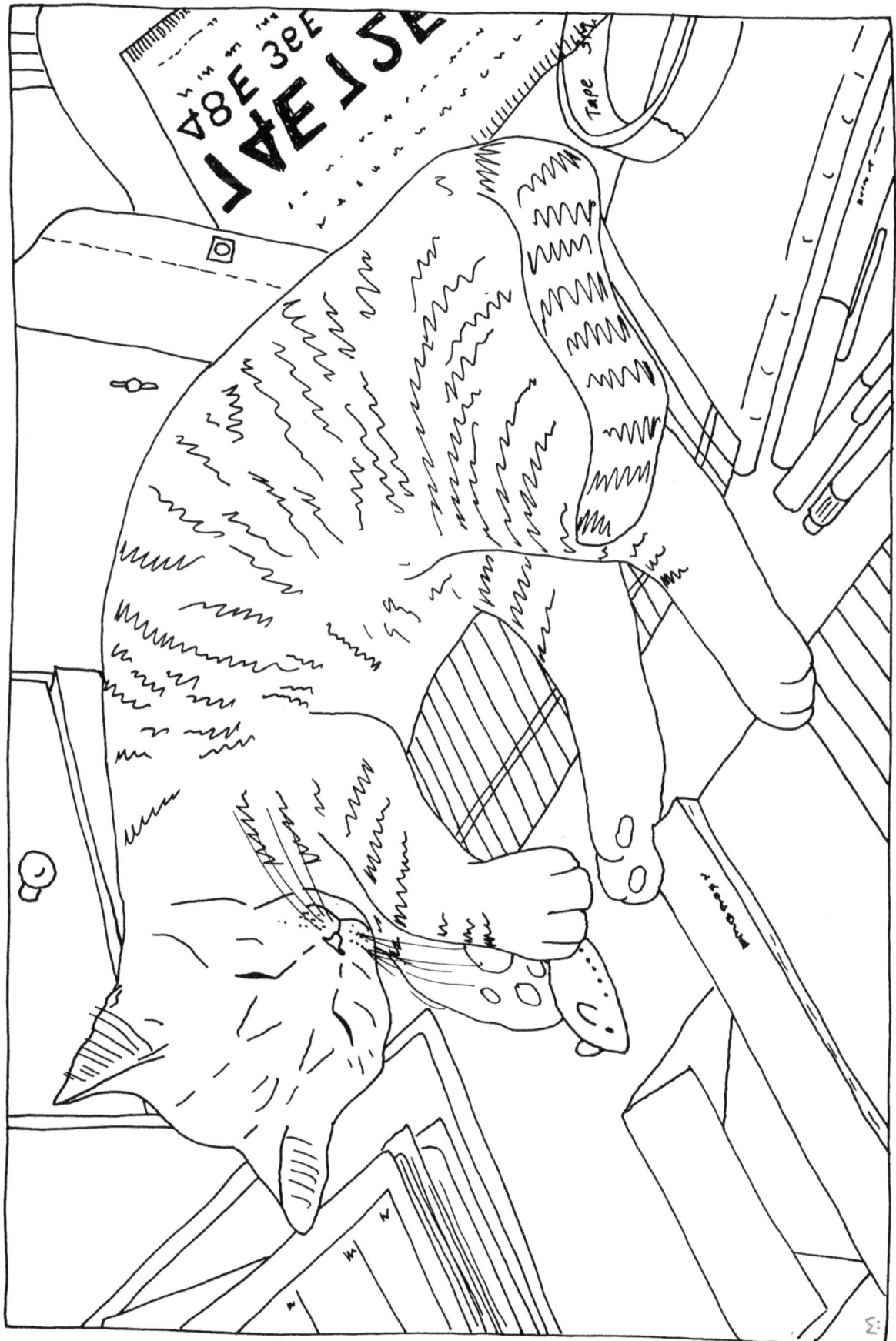

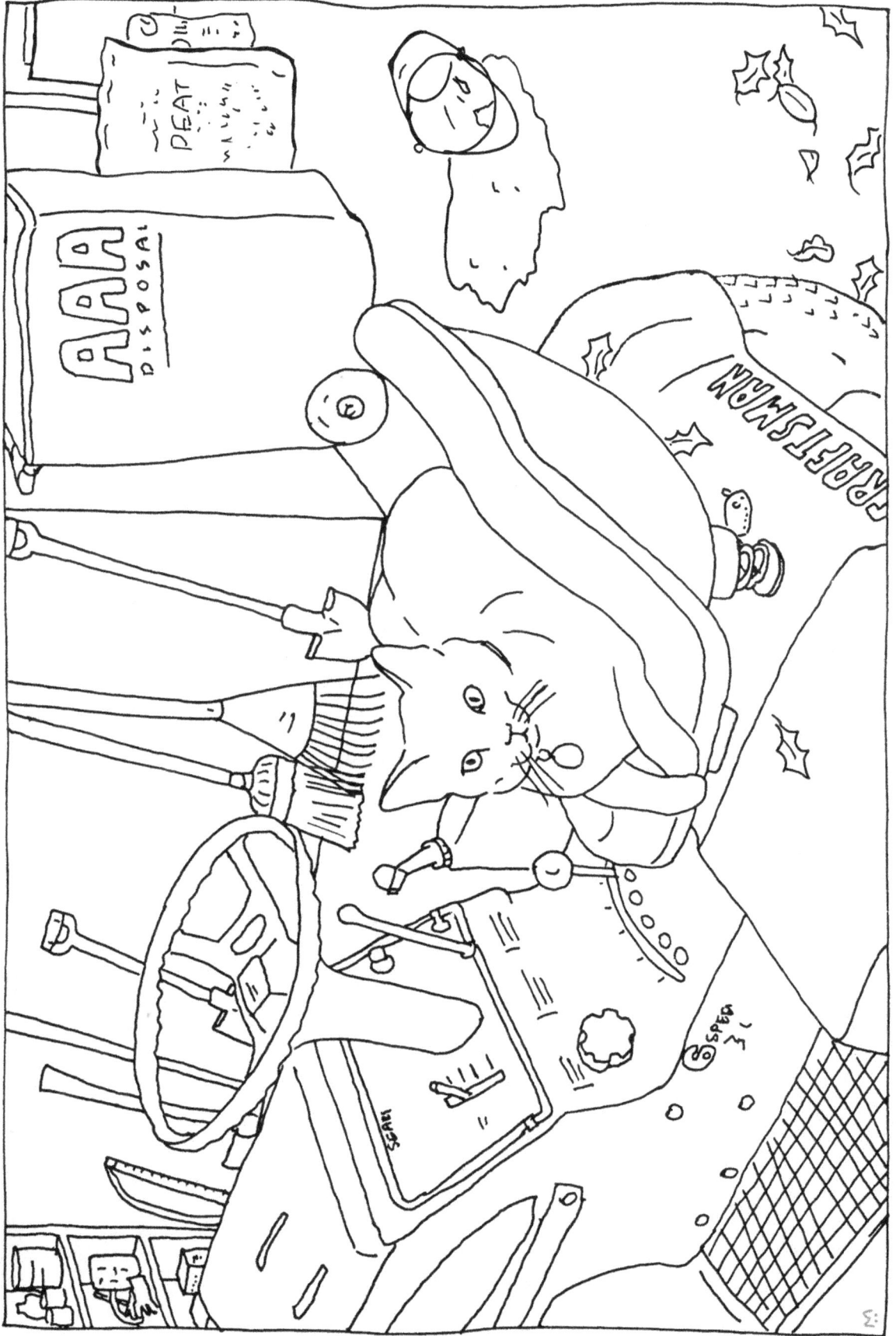

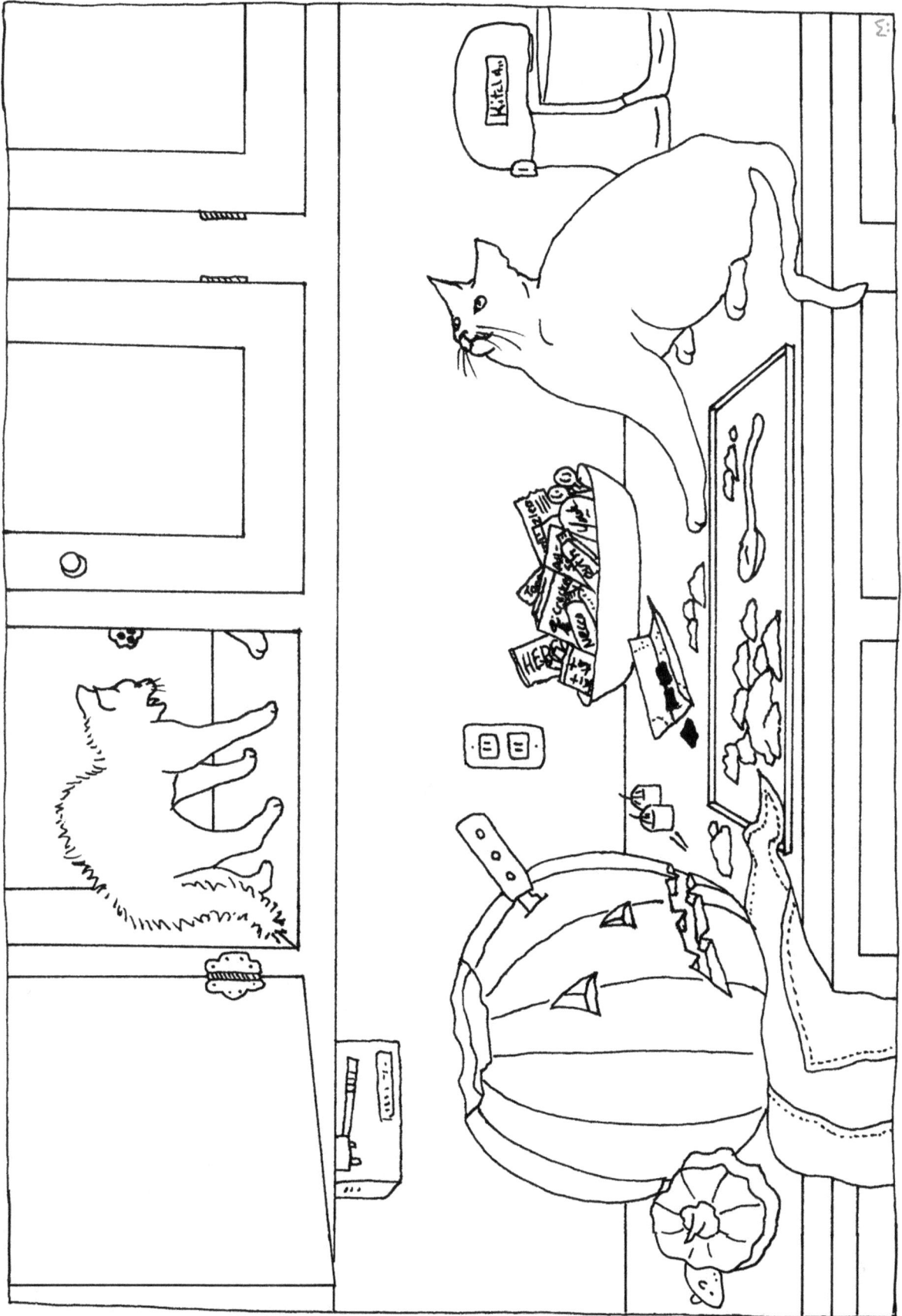

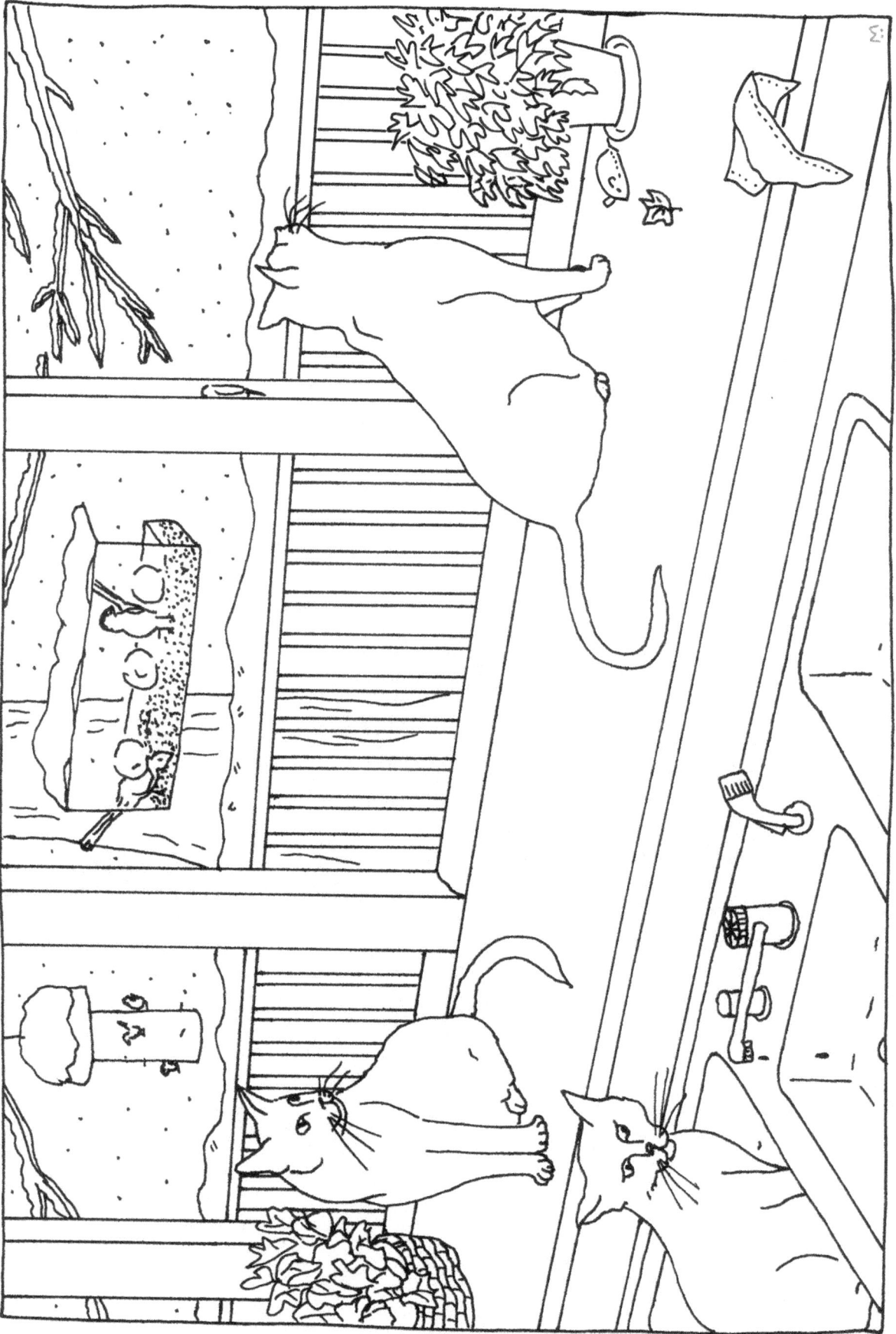

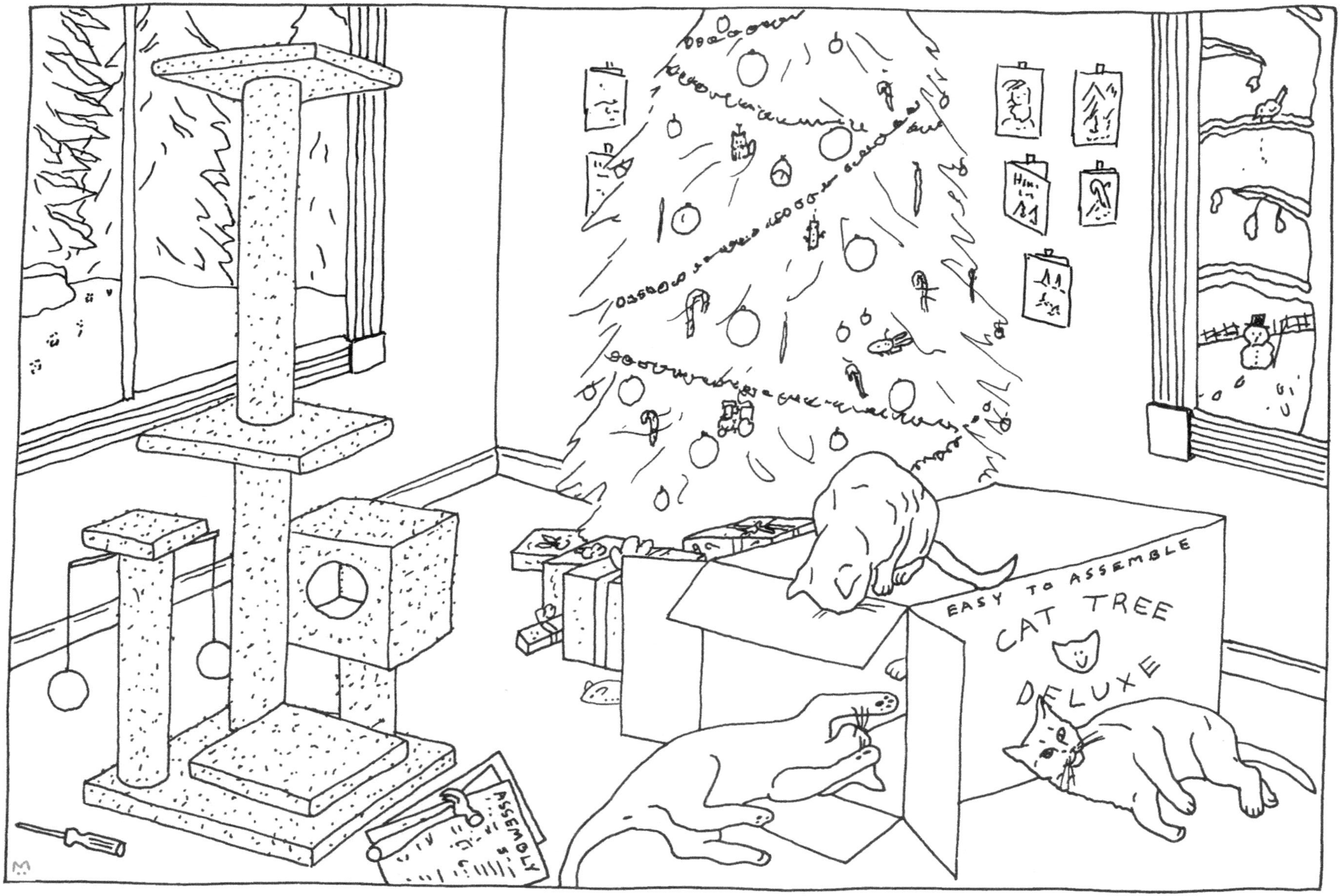
EASY TO ASSEMBLE
CAT TREE
DELUXE
ASSEMBLY

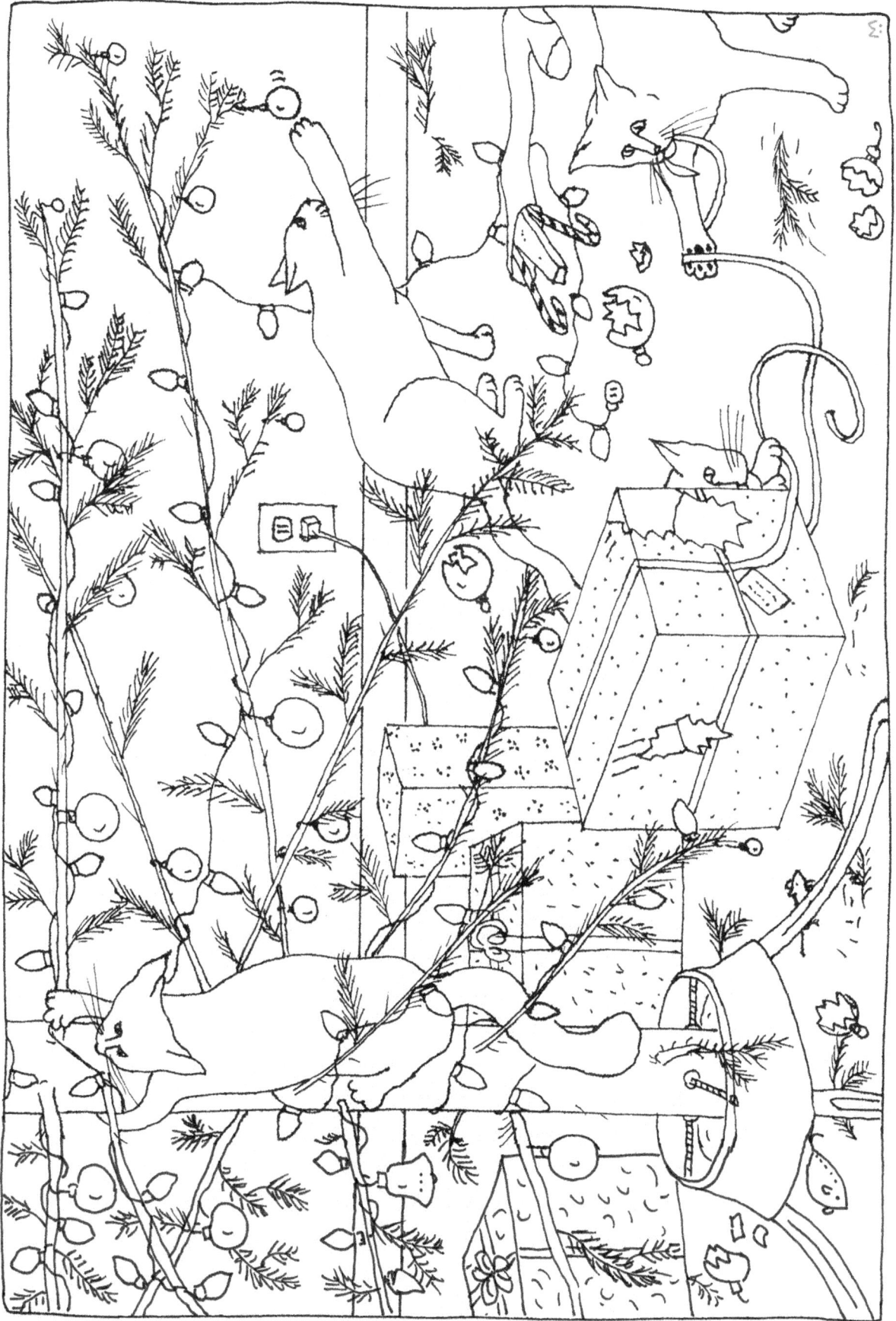

Margaret Gates Root is the founder of the
Feline Nutrition Foundation, a non-profit organization dedicated
to helping our feline companions lead healthier, happier lives by educating
pet parents on the benefits of bio-appropriate nutrition for cats.

For more information, visit the Foundation at
FelineNutritionFoundation.org